General Introduction Unbound Project 0

Printing and Social Change 1

The Effect of the Printed Book on Language in the 16th Century 2

The Argument: Causality in the Electric World
Marshall McLuhan and Barrington Nevitt 3

The Relation of Environment to Anti-Environment 4

At the Moment of Sputnik the Planet became a Global Theater
in which there are no Spectators but only Actors 5

Culture without Literacy 6

The Humanities in the Electronic Age 7

Introduction to: The Bias of Communication 8

American Advertising 9

Inside Blake and Hollywood **10**

G. K. Chesterton: A Practical Mystic 11

Roles, Masks and Performances 12

Space, Time and Poetry 13

New Media as Political Forms 14

Notes on the Media as Art Forms 15

The Media Fit the Battle of Jericho 16

The Medium is the Message 17

Myth and Mass Media 18

Laws of the Media 19

The Emperor's Old Clothes 20

Introduction by W. Terrence Gordon

This book review, published early in McLuhan's career (*Sewanee Review* 55, October 1947, pages 710-15), makes use of some of the broad-ranging material he gathered in preparation for writing his Ph. D. thesis (*The Place of Thomas Nashe in the Learning of his Time*, Cambridge University, 1943)*. Hence, for example, his allusion to "the medieval notion of the *translatio studii*, the continuous transmission of culture from Greece to Rome, from Rome to Britain, and from Britain to the court of Charlemagne." References such as this and to "the awareness of the mythopoeic activity in history and art" become less explicit in McLuhan's later writings, though they do not cease to be part of his own perspective or to be integrated in modified form in his analytical procedures and the implicit program of educational reform he will perpetually advocate. His idea of pairing Blake and Hollywood, high literature and popular culture, before they had separated, came before the *audiences* had separated. His opening sentences signal the inseparability of his concerns: "[The books under review] serve to remind us that one of the principal intellectual developments of the past century or so has been the supplanting of linear perspective by a multi-locational mode of perception." McLuhan's manifold teachings around this topic unified his entire career. Here the young professor displays his command of a remarkable range of studies; particularly noteworthy, in his opening paragraph, as a formative influence on McLuhan, is the reference to the magisterial work of his colleague Etienne Gilson, *The Unity of Philosophical Experience*. — WTG

---

* To be published in November 2005 by Gingko Press as *The Classical Trivium*

Inside Blake and Hollywood

by H. Marshall McLuhan

There is a sufficient similarity of approach to the subject in these two books [1] to justify their being bracketed for discussion. They serve to remind us again that one of the principal intellectual developments of the past century or so has been the supplanting of linear perspective by a multi-locational mode of perception. Among critics of Picasso this new mode is sometimes referred to as a "circulating point of view" in which a view from above may suddenly become a view from everywhere at once. When this mode appears in a work of philosophy (as it does for the first time in Etienne Gilson's *The Unity of Philosophical Experience*) the possibilities for compression and for the organic

1 *Fearful Symmetry: A Study of William Blake.* By Northrop Frye. Princeton University Press. 462 pp. $5.00. *Magic and Myth of the Movies.* By Parker Tyler. Henry Holt and Company. xx, 283 pp. $3.00.

interrelation of facts, pressures, and ideas is altogether a new thing. It represents a real advance in the tools of intellectual analysis. And that this new way of making and also of deciphering ideographs should be inseparable from the achievement of Vico and Freud is only natural. For it has come about through the awareness of the unity of mythopoeic activity in history and art, and it has given modern man a sense once more of the simultaneity of all history seen at the psychological and intellectual level, as well as of the close bonds between all members of the human family past and present.

Blake's view was that "history as linear time is the great apocrypha or mystery which has to be rejected" since "the whole of human life is seen and understood as a single mental form." (p. 340) The linear view of history began with Petrarch and Leonardo da Vinci and ended with Gibbon and Hume. So obsessive a metaphor as that of linear perspective is important enough to deserve some explanation, especially since we are now deep in the process of extricating ourselves from it. For it still holds firmly among such inheritors of eighteenth-century rationalism as the sociologists and the Marxists.

Briefly, the linear metaphor grew up in connection with the medieval notion of the *translatio studii*, the continuous transmission of culture from Greece to Rome, from Rome to Britain, and from Britain to the court of Charlemagne. So that Abelard could regard Paris in the twelfth century as the lineal descendant and sole legatee of Athens. This notion of a translatio studii, however, was curiously jolted by the quarrel which developed between the new scholastic theology and the traditional patristic or humanist theology. The quarrel began in the Twelfth Century between Abelard and St. Bernard. Two hundred years later Petrarch had reduced and confused the matter to merely nationalist terms. The schoolmen, whom he regarded as the barbarians or the Goths and Huns of learning, had met with no opposition outside Chartres, Orleans, and Italy. L. J. Paetow summed it up concisely: "Now the lowest ebb in the study of ancient classical literature occurred in the century which preceded Petrarch. So low it was that he and his contemporaries believed that the dry and barren period on which they had fallen must have extended back for centuries to the last days of classic Latin literature." It is only in this context that Petrarch's celebrated statement about his being a man placed between two ages makes any sense. And it is this passage which focuses that sense of linear perspective which still ruled the imagination of Gibbon.

Gilson discusses the entire question in chapter X of his revision of *La Philosophie au Moyen Age*, explaining in its context (p. 728) Petrarch's statement that he was "placed on the frontier of two peoples looking both backwards and forwards." The supposition has been that these "two peoples" were those of the Middle Ages and those of the Renascence — those of a dead past and a living future. But Petrarch refers to a living past and a dead future, exactly as Gibbon does. Behind him he saw a great antiquity followed by centuries which gradually relinquished the ancient inheritance. Before him he could see only a period in which the already dim and blurred memories of antiquity were to pass into a final night of oblivion.

Here, at any rate, is the origin of the metaphor of simple linear perspective which yields in Vico to a complex genetic metaphor that becomes the intellectual means of being simultaneously present in all periods of the past and all mental climates of the modern world as well. For Vico contains Wordsworth, Freud, and Malinowski by anticipation in answering the questions: "exactly how do people so remote in time or culture or condition as Lucy Gray or Ivanhoe or a neurotic or a Trobriander *feel*? What is the world they know?"

Professor Frye takes us inside Blake in this way. *Fearful Symmetry* supplants entirely the work of Middleton Murry and Foster Damon, and of the other exegetists of Blake. For having installed himself inside Blake he does a detailed job of exploration and is able to speak of current issues as we might suppose Blake would have spoken. And, indeed, "the voice of the bard" is heard with typical emphasis on most contemporary matters, artistic and political. It is at once clear that Blake was a great psychologist with clear insight into the mechanism of human motives and of historical periods — his own included. And his psychological insights grew into an all-embracing system which was nothing short of ferocious in its rationalistic completeness.

That is the paradox of Blake — that he so largely became the image of the thing he hated and fought, namely Lockean rationalism and abstraction. In Professor Frye's words (p. 143):

Blake was, it is obvious, so conscious of the shape of his central myth that his characters become almost diagrammatic. The heroism of Orc

> or the ululation of Ololon do not impress us as human realities, like Achilles or Cassandra, but as intellectual ideographs. It all depends on whether the reader has a taste for this kind of metaphysical poetry or not . . . what there is in Blake is a dialectic, an anatomy of poetry, a rigorously unified vision of the essential forms of the creative mind, piercing through its features to its articulate bones.

Unlike Vico and Joyce but like Freud, Blake mistook a psychology for metaphysics and theology. His rigorous monism had no place for "the many" save as modes of primal, divine energy. The created world is a part of fallen god-head and is essentially evil. Existence and corruption are the same. This makes for simplicity, intensity, and inclusiveness of outlook, but it may not have been of as much use to Blake the poet as he himself supposed. It made Blake an encyclopedic allegorist but it also led him to attach a final rather than a provisionary value to his allegorical imagery. That is, Blake was not so much concerned with the visual and dramatic character of his imagery as with its intellectual meaning. So that reading Professor Frye is a more satisfactory thing for most of Blake than reading Blake himself. The great poetical allegorist like Dante proceeds by simile, although the entire work is a huge metaphor. Blake proceeds by metaphor or identity of tenor and vehicle and ends up with a work which requires a key to open. His intellectual structure is not realized dramatically in the "major" poems but has to be set beside them. Professor Frye does not regard this as a defect since his business in his book is exegesis and not criticism (p. 359):

No student of Blake can fail to be deeply impressed by the promptness with which Blake seizes on the machine as the symbol of a new kind of human existence developing in his own time. His poetry is an imaginative mechanism designed to fight the machine age; it has the "wheels within wheels" of Ezekiel's vision which will reverse the direction of the "wheel without wheel with cogs tyrannic Moving by compulsion each other" . . .

Professor Frye's inside view of Blake in which every part of the bard's thought is seen to have a strict etiolation and coherence is perhaps in need of some further development from the outside. Blake is psychologically in the tradition of patristic allegory unbroken from Philo of Alexander to the Cambridge Platonists, and he needs to be closely compared and contrasted with Vico. But much gratitude is due to Professor Frye for having brought into a conclusive focus all the elements of Blake's thought and feeling.

Parker Tyler is the first American to give serious attention to popular culture as it is expressed by Hollywood, and Magic and *Myth of the Movies* is a sequel to *The Hollywood Hallucination*. Mr. Tyler substitutes perception for abuse or passivity — the only current attitudes to Hollywood as to all popular culture. Just how it has been possible for those who regard Joyce and Eliot with respect to exempt themselves from a rigorous evaluation of every phase of commercial culture is perhaps only to be explained by the obsession with mechanistic abstraction which an industrial society imposes. For example, the Ford motor company has in its museum working models of all locomotives and all motor cars ever made. But it has no records of production methods employed in the manufacture of its early cars — a fact which rightly shocked Sigfried Giedion. However, the kind of repercussion which every phase of the technological world may have on the artist and on the modes of our sensibility is illustrated frequently in Moholy-Nagy's *Vision in Motion.* Apropos of the seemingly disparate themes of Joyce and Ford cars, he points out on page 350, for example, that "one can find in Joyce's writings analogies to contemporary technological terms . . . manifolded word agglutinations (often constructed from German, Hungarian or other composites . . .) . . . similar to the industrial process of assemblage. . . ." Joyce, of course, was extremely conscious of scores of inter-related analogies in the modes of his artistic activity. And Eliot is explicit:

> It was here, in the kitchen in the passage,
>
> In the mews in the barn in the byre in the market place
>
> In our veins our bowels our skulls as well
>
> As well as in the plottings of potentates.

Committed to an atomistic conception of himself and society, the American intellectual doesn't really credit these things. Movies aren't *avant garde*; therefore they are insignificant. This, in a word, is why the *avant garde* has to be imported. So Mr. Tyler's books have been given a gentle brush-off in spite of his showing that vulgar and commercial entertainment is often of great psychological complexity and that there is nothing in high art which doesn't appear in some confused mode in low art.

A major postulate of Mr. Tyler is illustrated in his statement (pp. 255-256) that:

> The rudimentary camera trick, for instance, that of appearing and disappearing persons, which occurs in the wink of an eye, is a visualization of the correspondence between matter and spirit that was a cardinal tenet in the beliefs of primordial savages.

This sets *The Golden Bough* right in the Hollywood Bowl. It further implies that every mode of technology is a reflex of our most intimate psychological experience. The *pointillage* of Seurat is a derivative of Humean association psychology and exfoliates again in modern wire-photos. Movie technique has obvious relations with the panoramic devices of Scott or Tolstoy. And the close-up, as well as darkroom projection, can be traced back to the Rembrandt "point of light" school in the same way. If this should seem "merely mechanical" it can be shown that the entire conception of characterization in novel and drama since the mid-Eighteenth Century is similarly based on sensationalism divorced from any scheme of social and moral references. That is merely another point of view from which to observe the "picturesque" characters of modern fiction from Clarissa onwards. They stand in a palpitating focus of self-awareness.

It is in this sort of way that Mr. Tyler takes us inside Hollywood with its mushrooming symbolism. Exuberance of semi-conscious and uncontrolled symbols on one hand, and shrewd technical and commercial control on the other. For all the conscious intellectual activity of an industrial society is directed to non-human ends. Its human dimensions are systematically distorted by every conscious resource while the unconscious and commercially unutilized powers struggle dimly to restore balance and order by homeopathic means.

It is for this reason that Hollywood dominates the psychic life of America. It provides the night-dream which exorcises the terrors of the day-time actuality. Mr. Tyler's great merit is that he explores the multiple modes of the movie night-dream as it is his limitation seldom if ever to emerge from that dream. He is quite frank about his purpose not to "analyze the best movies as the *artistic best* but as the *mythological best*," and like Mr. William Empson he has no technique of evaluation of the products he explores. Nor does he consider many of the moral, social, or political wherefores of Hollywood's deep artistic anemia. Thus in discussing the anomalous excellence of S. Ansky's *The Dybbuk* he can find no criterion for placing the essential Hollywood impotence. He rightly finds *The Song of Bernadette* repulsive but his tools of analysis do not carry him to the point where he can isolate the *cliché* and timidity as rooted in the death of all intellectual impulse. This in turn is related to Mr. Tyler's lack of expressed awareness of the perennial uses and necessity of art in maintaining social viability. He does a fine job of reading the enigmas of the fever chart from the movies but of the positive function of popular art for good or ill he says nothing.

But this should not be too disturbing since there has been no lack of critics who have proclaimed the uplifting or degrading qualities of the movies without having noticed anything whatever of what was going on in them. Mr. Tyler is right, therefore, to concentrate attention on the complexity and eminent snideness of movie art as preliminary to opening up a plenary critique.

Inside Blake and Hollywood
Marshall McLuhan - Unbound (10)

ISBN: 1-58423-051-7
Library of Congress Control Number 2005927213

Marshall McLuhan Unbound Project Editors
Eric McLuhan, W. Terrence Gordon

Published in United States in October 2005 by
Gingko Press, Inc.
5768 Paradise Drive, Suite J • Corte Madera, CA 94925
(415) 924-9615 • Fax (415) 924-9608
email: books@gingkopress.com
http://www.gingkopress.com

Design, packaging and production: Die Gestalten Verlag, Berlin
Layout and Typography: onlab, Berlin
Fonts: *Dolly* by Underware, *Bullet* by House Industries
Production: Martin Bretschneider, Vinzenz Geppert
Art direction: Robert Klanten

Made in Germany